Also by Granger T Barr

Table of Contents

HAUNTED HOSPITALS

True Real Hospital Ghost Stories & Hauntings

25 Unexplained Supernatural Mysteries Of The Paranormal

In Britain And America

Granger T Barr

The storytellers have been granted permission to use these stories. However, their identities have been changed so as not to be identified.

Introduction

———

Medical personnel and patients mainly from Britain, the United States of America, and a few places in Europe share their terrifying, genuine stories of paranormal activity in hospitals, hospices, and nursing homes.

Sit back, relax and enjoy these 25 real-life, true tales.

Resident Spirit

―――

We have a haunted room with only eight mattresses, two on the right and six on the left, and a nurse workstation in the middle.

I was chatting with the nurses at the hospital desk early one morning when I noticed from the corner of my eye

this older gentleman, slowly walking into the final room

I started running towards him because no one should stand or walk unaided. Finally, I got to the room. It was empty, and only then did I realise that we had no patients in that room. Then, I turned around, and I went back to the nurse's room, where everyone was smiling at me. I asked them, "*Did you see another patient in the bed?*". The nurses giggled at me, and one nurse said, "*Honey, you made us laugh the way you ran. So, now you have met our resident ghost; we haven't seen him in a long while, not until today.*"

Everyone in the hospice would say this to newbies. They would reassure them that the old gentleman would only introduce himself to people he liked, which meant I was now initiated and entirely accepted as a team member.

The Oncology Unit

I work in an adult oncology unit where, unfortunately, we have a lot of comfort care patients.

Most of them would transition to a hospice where they sometimes live out their final days, don't make it, and pass away while they're still in the hospital or rather the hospice.

Naturally, we have the most deaths in the hospice unit, and many don't really like coming up to the floor because everyone dies. But, all staff love the place, and there is so much love between all the nurses and our patients. We get to know them well. When people pass away, we notice that, not surprisingly, it comes in threes, as they say.

There are weeks when no one dies. Everyone pulls out of there and onto a hospice or another facility, where they choose where to die. They usually have only a week or two to have three to six deaths inside a week.

We had two patients pass away one night; one patient was still roommates. So, it was a challenging time for all involved.

She had been on the floor for a lengthy period as we all watched her go from a spry old lady to wasting away in all aspects. Then, finally, she passed at night, and by the next day, there was a new patient in her room; it was hard on us all, and we all know patients come and go, and we have to move on.

I admitted the new patient and went over room orientation stuff. I explained that she had a one-stop-shop remote control, which controlled: the lights; tv, radio and the call light.

Right, so as I finished explaining to her that the tv buttons were right here, I placed the remote down on her bed, and instantly the tv turned on all by itself.

But then, it began flipping through each channel at an alarming rate, faster than if you were to hold down the channel up button.

The lady was a little older and thankfully was not very observant, and she imagined I was doing it, but I said I was not touching it at all.

I didn't want the tv on right now, so I reached down and tried to turn it off, but it didn't turn off! So I ended up panicking. Unfortunately, the TV still wouldn't turn off after I unplugged the remote from the wall, and typically, it would be all connected and not working if it wasn't appropriately plugged. So I had to shut off the TV in the end manually.

I left the room and told her I'd be right back, and as I went to the nurse's desk to grab another one, I ran into another nurse who was holding another remote, which was odd. I just got a new delivery in, and they were all usually working correctly.

We rarely had to replace them anymore, and I asked the other nurse if her remote was broken too? And she said hers was acting up. I then asked the nurse which room she was in, but it was a different room that a patient had died the night before.

Also, the TV remote controls were uncharacteristically playing up from across the wing; simultaneously, people died in the same rooms the previous night.

How freaky? I could ramble on about this forever. Still, most stories are related to TV.

The TV Remote Volume

―――――

A nother disturbing situation is similar to what I previously described, whereby the remote control changes channels. I have a problem whereby the TV volume kept increasing and decreasing in a patient's room recently passed on.

I've also noticed lights not work and then worked again. I had even seen a sink tap turn itself on when no one else was around. We have several designated rooms reserved for our comfort care patients, and even when they are occupied, we will walk by them, and it feels like someone's in there, but when we look, it's empty.

We have a room where pumps stop working, machines quit on us, and nothing seems to work. But that room got cleansed by a priest saying prayers, which I know sounds crazy, but since then, everything in the room has worked fine.

I've never been a massive believer in the paranormal or supernatural, but it's not hard to believe after working on this unit for the past year.

We embrace it now because what else can you do?

Never Alone

———

I'm a nurse, walked down the hallway, and went into the clean utility room to get a warm blanket. Someone was walking ahead of me about six to eight feet. Unfortunately, I could not tell you much about them or what they even looked like.

Still, I remember thinking a staff member opened the door to the clean utility, which requires a punching code. And it shut before I got to it; mildly annoyed that they didn't hold it open for me, I opened the door, but no one was in there. So I thought it was weird but didn't tell anyone about it or think much of it. But, later that night, my co-worker and I were chatting about our shift, and the nurse then said, "*oh, and yeah, it seems we have a ghost*".

I asked her what she meant by that statement? She went on to clarify the same as my experience, except it had been told to her by another co-worker. It was in the hallway; the same clean utility. And the same feeling of it being a staff member. But he also couldn't tell you any descriptive details at all.

Over the last year, it has occurred to three more people.

No TV, Please!

———

So the lady in room 240 hated the TV in her room. She lived there for years and would yell at roomies that turned on their TV.

She would also fall asleep holding the button on her call bell to annoy us. Finally, one day she died in the middle of the night while I was not there, and the nurse on duty at the other station reported the automatic front doors opening for no reason.

It was later discovered that there were a low census moments after her death, so her room remained empty; nursing assistants would frequently go into 240 and watch the TV on their breaks. They reported that the TV would often turn off for no reason as they watched it; her call bell would go off without

anyone being in the room for months

after her death. This was an old building with faulty wiring, but it was still very creepy.

Scream Of Terror

———

I'm a nurse on duty tonight and have some spooky stories about two travel nurses working in the United States, and they decided to drive out of town.

Unfortunately, they had a bad accident, and one of them died. That night she died; the staff heard a terrorising scream throughout the hospital she had worked.

It was so loud that the nurses checked room by room in multiple units to see where it came from; a day or two later, everyone found out about the nurse's death; the accident was the same time everyone heard the scream.

The Young Girl

———

A nother story was in an isolation room with another room separated by a solid door and then a door with a window.

A patient-reported to her nurse that a young girl kept staring at them through the door window. She even entered the room and went into the bathroom to sit in the tub!

The patient said they could hear water running and suddenly switch off. She was too terrified to move and waited all night for the girl to come out of the bathroom, but she never did.

When the duty nurse came around the following day, the patient told the nurse someone was in the bathroom.

The nurse knocked on the door, listened and then opened it slowly. The bathroom was empty, and the bathtub was dry.

The Staircase

———

The last story is about stairs which is an excellent way to get some exercise and keep you awake while on duty.

We have eight floors, so not too bad, but unfortunately, sometimes you get a horrible feeling when using the stairs in the middle of the night.

Sometimes it feels like someone is on the stairs with you. You could even occasionally hear noises, so now the stairs are avoided at night.

Sometimes, the elevator will stop on our floor and open if someone presses the button, but there's no one inside.

No one pressed the button.

Long Term Care Unit

I work in the long-term care unit, and we have tons of stories to tell. I'll give you two of my favourite ones.

We used to have a lady in our assisted living unit. She was a lovely dear older woman with dementia who could never understand how to use her call switch for assistance.

As a result, she would walk over to her next-door neighbour's apartment every night and ask him to assist her in getting ready for bed.

He'd then activate his call light and inform whoever was on duty that the lady needed assistance.

The older man is still with us, and he has no cognitive deficits or memory issues. He's here because of severe liver and kidney problems and can't manage all of his tubes and medication.

The lady next door to him became ill with pancreas issues and stopped knocking on the man's door for about a month. Unbeknown to him, she had sadly passed away.

As usual, at approximately eight that night, while the family was still in the ladies' apartment room next door, the older man put on his call light and said that the lady next door was ready for bed. Creepy right, the CNA figured out that he was picking up on an old routine.

Hence, the unit assistant asked him had the older lady had come here to him? He explained that she must have softly tapped on the door because he didn't hear her knock.

He reported that the older lady next door was wearing a white robe and holding her rosary beads in her hands. She kept whispering to herself as if she was praying.

The CNA then told the older man what had happened. He said, "*I being*

a huge sceptic, didn't believe it". He said he must have been dreaming!

The lady's family finally left next door, and when the funeral home director arrived to take the body, he said he

went out next door to help move her

onto the cart. The older man said when they walked into the room, there she was, lying in bed with the exact same white gown, rosary beads in hand.

The neighbour still occasionally puts on

his light for her.

The Old Nursing Home

———

In the following story, my building sits on the same site as the old nursing home in our town. A non-profit agency purchased it, tore it down and rebuilt it into the building I currently work in.

The old building had an amiable woman who worked in the old kitchen as a cook. She had worked there until she finally retired.

A few years later, the ex-cook had a stroke and came to live in the new building. Unfortunately, she had vascular dementia, too and pretty severely. She would find her way into the kitchen most of the time, and we had to lead her back to her room.

She eventually died about a year ago; strange things would happen in this kitchen since she passed.

You can often hear fridge doors open and slam closed!

One of the staff was getting chips, but when she said the large freezer door came open, she watched a dark smoke-like outline walk out, stop, and turn to her, wave and disappear. She didn't go back into the kitchen after that. I offered her a hundred bucks once, and she point blank refused.

The Pregnancy

―――――

M y wife was expecting a baby, and we had our c-section scheduled early because she has polyhydramnios, and our son was measuring 9 pounds and 35 weeks. He was only born 6 pounds, though. We decided to attend it because it was only a few blocks away from our home.

It was ancient and very institutional

looking building, and the maternity unit had one very long hallway with rooms on either side. The nurse's station was in the middle of where our son was born, and we spent the next three days in the unit where we came up to the department.

We suddenly noticed another couple was in one of the birthing suites at the opposite end of the hallway from us. We heard babies crying every day at

entirely appropriate intervals for the

duration of our stay. They would cry for three to four minutes every one to two hours every day like clockwork.

Finally, when we got discharged home, we asked the nurse if the other couple on the unit had a boy or a girl?

The nurse gave us a mystified look and told us that we were the only couple there.

Well, if we have another child, we'll go to a different hospital next time.

Miscarriages

My wife has had three miscarriages since our son was born on Christmas day. There is a cemetery at the hospital where the unborn babies are buried.

It was snowing the night heavily before, so the entire grounds were covered with fresh white snow.

We couldn't drive into the cemetery yet because it hadn't been ploughed, so we decided to park on the roadside.

This is a very rural area, and the cemetery had perhaps one hundred plots. When we strolled into the graveyard, we observed a single set of very tiny footprints of a child's that led us through the gate and intertwined through the gravestones, directly to the spot where our babies were buried.

The footprints did not turn around, go back, or lead anywhere else in the cemetery! The footprints simply appeared to that burial spot and stopped.

The moment we arrived at that very spot our babies were buried, it started to snow again with the most king-size beautiful snowflakes I've ever seen. We said a little prayer, and my wife cried. We then walked back to our car, and it stopped snowing by the time we got back to the vehicle. How crazy is that?

Wondering Outside The TV Room

One evening I was still on duty. I told the receptionist that I'd cover the desk for the time being while she took her break and because it was right outside the Common or TV room.

Suddenly, someone approached me from around the corner of the corridor; as I was sorting cardiac rhythm strips out of nowhere, the man indicated he was seeking the exit.

But I noticed he was still clothed in the hospital gown wearing a bracelet. So I asked him for his room number as I looked up to see him standing there, in front of me.

I told him to wait at the desk while I went and called the PCA to come downstairs for him. I gave her his room number, but she informed me that it couldn't be the correct room because the patient in that room had died about 20 minutes ago. She wondered if it was a family member, perhaps? Chillingly, I told her no.

I returned to the reception desk, but he had vanished.

Mirror Mirror

I met a perfectly healthy and balanced woman; we got talking. I discovered her and relocated and moved in with her fiancé.

According to her fiancé, their brand-new home was haunted. Their things were being moved about or missing, and doors were slamming shut and unusual, strange sounds were heard during the night.

Her fiancé came home one night from work and found her crying by the restroom mirror. I asked her why she was so stunned, and she claimed she was exhausted could not recall very much but fell asleep and went to bed. Although she had awakened, she felt like she could not take a breath. Her fiancé took her to the hospital emergency.

She was later transferred to another room for a surgical procedure. Her fiancé was so worried and waited for her to come out later. Finally, they moved her to a room on the second floor.

I noticed her bed was at the opposite end to a mirror. You sit up in bed; you can see your reflection in the mirror, which often makes patients feel uncomfortable and is not that unusual of a demand to have a bed sheet taped over to cover it up.

Early one morning, the nurse bathed her and got her up into the chair they do baths. I may have dropped off to sleep in the recliner.

The nurse left to obtain additional sheets to cover the mirror but may have gotten side-tracked and failed to remember all about leaving the woman in the room alone with the exposed mirror.

The telephone call bell goes off a little while later on, and after realising her slip up, the nurse goes to get a sheet, but when she entered the room, she found to her sheer terror that the lady was dead on the flooring, with her test tube torn right out.

Don't Believe In Ghosts But...

———

Some of these stories I've heard about haunted rooms and units come from reliable sources, and once from my own when I was a nurse assistant, we had 47 on the other floor a small child haunted that on numerous occasions patients in this room would hit the call light and ask us to get these kids out of my room.

One night a patient called out and asked me to shut his door because kids laughed in the hallway. But, of course, it was late, and no kids were on the floor.

I just apologised and shut the door five minutes later. He called and asked us to get the little girl in his room out because she was at the foot of his bed. So, I went in there, and he said that she was gone but that she'd been staring at him.

These things happened several times over my three years working there.

I never witnessed the second story but had actual interactions with ghosts and spirits while working at the hospital in south London. It was on the second floor was an overflow where the central unit got full but had eight beds in it.

Allegedly, a nurse that had worked in the hospital a long time ago and a patient had died in one room opposite the nurse's desk. So it wasn't easy to see while sitting at the desk. One night, the nurse was on the telephone when she saw another nurse walk into that room out of the corner of her eye.

She got curious after a few minutes because the room was empty, and she assumed someone went in there and got cords or something. So she got up and went in, but there was no one in the same room.

A nurse went in early in the morning to change a patient's dressing. The patient was zero times out of ten entirely with it but was confused about why the nurse was doing dressing changes.

The patient stated there was another nurse in here 10 minutes ago

that changed my dressing, thinking it was the other nurse in the unit that night as there were only two. She thanked the other nurse, who said she hadn't changed any dressings and had done something with her patient for several minutes.

Other stories happened, but they always took place in room two when only two nurses worked that unit.

The Night Shift

———

I was working in an oncology unit where it's not uncommon to have hospice patients back. When I was working, I hung out at the back with other nurses near the oncology rooms and studied for the next exam using dim lights at night. One prolonged night when the oncology rooms were all empty

I suddenly heard a clicking sound while I was reading. When patients are usually misusing a walker, there is a distinct sound against the floor tiles. And you know that someone is walking. So, I looked up to see which of the medical patients was awake and walking around, only to see no one there. So, I got up to investigate what was going on.

I approached the first three rooms, and the clicking sound was not coming. Then, as I approach the doorway of the fourth room, the clicking sound gets louder, and when I get to the entrance, the clicking stops.

I gave up my search, and then I returned to my studies. A few minutes later, the clicking sound resumed. I reapproach the doorway to the third room, and it stops again.

I head back to my studies, clicking resumes before even sitting down. I decided to check the rest of the rooms rather than trying the third room again

the clicking continues.

So, I'm reapproaching the third room the

clicking stops at this point. It's feeling a bit creepy now, and I'm just assuming my mind is playing tricks on me because I was rather tired.

Then I decided to go up to the front of the

a unit to join the other nurses who were chatting. I didn't think anything more of it, that is, until a few nights later.

A few nights after the event, my team had a busy, rather hectic night shift. The other nurses and I was still prepping our exams. I was the only aide on my particular floor, and the other nurses were busy too.

There was a big commotion during this significant shift. It was so crazy.

The family of a confused patient chose to leave for the night, causing their grandma to set off the bed alarm, and she's too unsteady to be up without

Assistance. She's also too confused to use her walker, and she's thinking she's back in her own house and trying to clean the house with a duster so, she's moving about in and out of her room, in the corridors, moving in ways that are making her more likely to fall.

After a few hours of this fiasco and several attempts to get grandma back inside her room, several calls were made to the doctor by the charge nurse and house officer of the patient.

I'm now sitting with a confused patient and an old duster, and the nurses are exhausted at this point. It's about midnight now, and the nurses are either charting or working on their midnight med pass. The room I'm sitting in is close enough to the nurses' station that I can hear the system when other

patients call, while confused grandma continues with her jumbled ramblings and odd behaviour. I hear a bathroom alarm ring on the cool light system when a patient pushes the call button, and the system beeps once every one to two seconds when the patient pulls the bathroom cord for assistance getting off the toilet. The system beeps four times a second the majority of patients' falls occur in the bathroom hence the more annoying sound to direct priority. The bathroom alarm continues to ring and ring, and I wonder why the hell aren't the nurses answering the call light? I ask myself, where the hell are they all?

The nurses carry small portable phones, which ring with the call lights. Perhaps the phones are not working. It happens. What felt like 20 minutes later, the bathroom alarm is still ringing, and at this point, I'm surprised there hasn't been a fall announced.

At last finally, the nurse comes into the room, and I tell her that I'll go back as long as I'm out of the room with grandma; the nurses can't leave so the patient can still be safe.

As soon as I step outside of the room, I realise that I do not hear the call light system; I hear a telephone in one of the patient's rooms loudly. It's not a ring like a pickup ring but rather a non-stop ring, one that I've never heard.

The ring sound is coming from the opposite direction of the nurse's station; it's coming from down the hall in the oncology room, not just any room but the furthest room.

I begin heading towards the sound, and as I get to the oncology rooms, they're all dark and absent of patience as I approach the room in question.

I can see the phone light up as it continues its drawn-out ring. As I step out of the room, I feel a cold shiver go down my spine, and I physically shudder. I've never felt this feeling before in my life.

As I walked across the room, I felt someone staring at the back of my head, and it felt as though someone was pouring out every ounce of hatred and rage into that stare.

Words honestly cannot describe or do justice to explain the feelings directed at me. As I walk around the empty bed, I pick up the phone, slam it down, and run out of the room! As soon as I cross the threshold, I feel physically relieved outside, and no hatred or rage is directed at me.

I quickly walked back to our boiler's chamber and let the nurse finish her med

pass. Unfortunately, it was not the last time I dealt with this nasty feeling of a ghost or an entity in that room. Occasionally when I have to go into the room to grab extra equipment or a chair, I could feel the angry presence.

Fortunately, the thing is usually pretty dormant whenever there's a patient in the room, not always, but usually.

I've had a few patients complain about not being able to sleep at night or relax in that room in particular or, they would complain about nightmares. But, once and thankfully, only once, the malevolence could even be felt during the day on a few occasions. I've sent co-workers into

the room for various reasons, and then

they have told me afterwards about the room. Most of them have agreed that something doesn't feel quite right in there.

The first hospital I worked at had a haunted room, and it wasn't a room. It was a larger mini-unit with four beds and monitors used as a higher acuity area. The blue call light would go on and off when no one was in it, and biomedical had checked out several

times but couldn't find anything wrong with the system. And after replacing it completely, it still happened; equipment and people's items would go missing and turn up in there. Things would randomly fall over and move around. Several patients asked to be moved out of that room because they complained it was cold no matter what the thermostat the setting was.

But the scariest one happened to me when I had a dementia patient in that very same room, and while I was settling her for the night, she turned to me and asked to "*please close the door because of that scary man who keeps watching me*".

New Building

O ur hospital opened up a brand new building. During the transition of the ICU theatres, radiology and four wards being moved, I worked in as part of the move. In addition, we opened up an emergency short-stay unit, an eight-bed unit for patients who were expecting to discharge in under 24 hours.

However, no one was admitted under a surgical or the medical team could stay in a ward environment until they're good to go home.

The elderly that have often come to us at night reported that life at home, alone with chest pains and waiting for a six-hour test to stable patients or awaiting transfer to a bigger hospital, was often on their minds.

Anyway, I've just finished a run of night shifts, and each shift, the nurse has reported things out of the ordinary the first few nights. One was a small unmounted whiteboard for patients names sliding off the desk and onto the floor. The following two nights, another registered nurse allocated there

reported that one of the cardiac monitors on standby had just come back on, on its own. It turns out

that in the three months that we had the new unit, we've already had a patient die there. One nurse remembered

running a patient from the unit

back into recess with an airway

in and the patient passing away, with no family members insight.

Another nurse recalled the feeling of being followed by some dark entity in the car park. She said she felt a strong presence when she got into her car and drove home a ten-minute drive. She felt very cold up to her front door.

When she got inside her house, she noticed a shadowy figure leaving the pathway, by the bushes, outside her porch. It was not human, and it was dark and smoky looking.

The Last Place I Worked

The last place I worked in other wards in Germany had a six-hour room where dead patients would stay for six hours before being checked for signs of death and moved to the morgue still attached to the hospital as it's a reasonably large one.

I'm not sure if this is a thing in other countries, but the patients are supposed to have a call-line within reach if they wake up and are not dead.

So there are about five to six call lines in the run anyway, and we had a fair number of patients dying, waiting in that room usually during the night shift. The light would switch on by itself from that room, even without any patients in there. So you'd have to go down and then turn them off again, and then they'd go on again just as you left the room bizarre as hell.

I never liked going down there alone, and it felt tense thick in the atmosphere. We reported the light issue to technicians who came and checked the connections and stuff like that, but everything worked fine without any problems.

The Catholic Hospital

———

I used to work in a Catholic hospital

before and after it was bought by a

larger health care system

while I didn't witness any of these

things myself I do have two first-hand accounts of an incident involving a nun that committed suicide back before I was born. The nuns were very active at the hospital. They started the health care in our area, and the hospital continued to grow back in the 70s or early 80s.

One day, a nun decided to jump off the building and take her own life; this caused quite an ordeal due to the catholic church.

A family member of mine was employed at the hospital and had a window office; she was working in her office when she saw a significant black figurine soaring and fall past her window. It was the nun.

Fast forward several years later, a supervisor on the night shift was making her rounds in the hospital.

She entered a long hallway with only windows on one side, and the hospital itself was probably 40 to 50 feet in length

with doors on either end, but no doors

opposite the windows. As she was midway down the hallway, she sensed something behind her and turned around. She witnessed a nun behind her and, thinking nothing of it. She simply said, "Oh, hello," before continuing down the hallway. Then, suddenly, she stopped as the realisation hit her; she then realised the nun was floating behind her. The woman instantly turned back around to an empty hallway. The hospital doors are very loud when you

open them. She didn't hear any doors opening allowing anyone to leave the hallway; this hallway was just below where the nun had decided to end her life.

Abandoned Hospital

There was an abandoned hospital near my grandma's town; it was a tuberculosis hospital, and many people died there, but the bodies were never claimed, so they were buried in unmarked graves behind the hospital

from the people I had spoken to in the

town was a miserable place to work

some of the staff suffered from mental

illness, one of the nurses ended her own life in the isolation ward in the 50s. Shortly after that, the hospital was shut

down. It would be rented out to host

gatherings and events but quickly fell

apart people reported screaming wheelchairs moving around doors opening and closing, and strangers coming from the building when I was younger; I remember checking it out. We didn't go inside, but we heard squeaking and screaming. Keep in mind the nearest houses were kilometres away, and it was up in the hills. We always got a creepy feeling when we passed by it like we were being watched, then one night in mid-2008, the hospital mysteriously caught fire.

The gas lines and powers had been disconnected since the mid-70s, and an investigation revealed that it was not caused by arson. No one had any knowledge about the actual cause of the fire, but the belief is that it was the work of the souls trapped inside.

The Elderly Patient

———

I was looking after an elderly patient, a very, very elderly patient, the oldest person I've ever taken care of. I don't remember why she was admitted, but it was minor, and she was due to go home the next day.

She was a very sharp lady, and she and I were having a friendly little chat. Then, while I was getting ready to wrap things up, the old lady said to me, "*I just want you to know who that little girl is standing behind you*".

The hair on the back of my neck raised. I ran through a quick assessment again on her. She knew which hospital she was in, yet she saw invisible children! I assured her there was no one else in the room. She was very non-plussed about it. I then went out to the nurse's station and enquired if my patient hallucinated about ghost children? Please help my conversation with my charge nurse, and she says, "*Are they in room 176? Yeah, I figured she's the second or third person who we've seen witness children in that room*".

The Security Guard

———

I used to work night security as a patrolman in this old hospital. Our cubicle was set up outside the hospital as it was all fenced off, but it was pretty famous for people to try urban exploring within it, as you can imagine.

Our task was to ensure that people never got in the first place; we had a whole section of cameras in our little unit where we could see pretty much anyone coming in or out of some blind spots.

We were supposed to go out and walk the perimeter every hour, which we did. It would only be one of us. But, of course, the night shift is when these people tend to come to do their exploring. The hospital itself didn't have much interest in it had been abandoned for so many years, but papers, desks, chairs, and the like persisted within its walls. It was a damp, dusk, and humid place, pretty much one of the worst places you could want to work.

Still, fortunately for me, I only had to be in there about 10 minutes every hour. I had only been working there a few months at this point. Nothing remotely interesting had happened other than having to ferry out some teenagers who thought they'd try and smash the window.

I caught them by chance walking my usual route, and instead of calling the cops, I saw their terrified faces on their 14 years old bodies and told them to leave and spoke that if they ever returned, there'd be severe consequences. After that, I never saw them again.

Not unless they broke in without me noticing, so as I'm doing the usual patrol, I have to go into the building, there are a couple of doors, but they're all locked. So the only ones we tend to use are the main entrance we go in, and just to the left are stairs that take us up every part of the hospital.

So we have to go through and around and back to this central section to go up to the next floor as the other stairs are locked and have stayed locked for a long time.

So, I'm doing the usual rounds of the five floors on the third floor and am pretty bored listening to a podcast when I hear something behind me.

Now to set the scene, I have a flashlight. Unfortunately, it's incredibly dark because the windows have been partially boarded up, and any external light is only vaguely creeping through. I just about crapped a brick.

There should be no one in here with me, and there is now, and that's fear-inducing; as I spin my flashlight around, I quickly glance, but there's no one.

I turn off my podcast and keep walking around in silence, and I stand there for a few minutes, seeing if I can see the light or hear someone. But, when I don't, I just call out security show yourself, but there's still no one. Slightly discouraged, I tell myself that if there is someone in here, they've got no way of escaping as I

didn't lock the door as I came in

so they'd either have to knock and beg

to come out, or I'll see them in the next

hour.

So, I make my rounds up to the fifth floor, and nothing's happening, but just as I made my way to the second floor and I'm descending the stairs, do I hear something on the second floor as well, on the doors to the right of me like a

wind that had caused the doors to swing ever so slightly. So, I peek through the glass into the gloom of the second floor and see nothing, but it's my job, so I push the doors open, shine my flashlight around and quickly peek to see if I can see anyone hidden behind some of the beds or chairs or something there's nothing.

I do complete the sweep of the second floor one more time as there's no way there was someone in there who had nowhere else to find no one. I'm freaking out at this point. I start making my way back, but before I hit the door, there's a small curtain that I can hide behind. So I decided that I was going to turn off my flashlight and hide there for a few minutes, listening to see if there was someone there.

I'm not going to lie. The moment I turned my flashlight off and felt the gloom and darkness overcome me, I genuinely felt quite scared, which I usually don't think on my job.

I waited to see if I could hear any signs of life. And after about five minutes of pure boredom and fear, I get up, and just as I'm about to turn my flashlight on, I hear a giggle from behind the curtain!

I instinctively punched the curtain, but it didn't travel very far, so it didn't get hit if someone was behind. I burst through it and looked around the empty room; there was no one here.

I do one more thorough sweep, this time believing that Satan and his minions have come to claim my soul bricking every step but didn't find a damn the thing I go back to my little hut and don't work at least not inspect the inside for the remainder of the day or the next day.

When I was speaking to my relief, I asked them if they'd seen anyone or heard anything unusual in the building, which was the first time I'd ever asked such a question. My then relief asks me if I'm referring to the ghost? And so I casually say that I didn't know what he was talking about the proceeds to tell me that others have reported seeing and hearing a small child within the hospital walls on different floors and that it's pretty playful and excitable.

So, to not buy into their nonsense, I give him a hearty laugh and tell him that I agree with him, and he's on his way home.

Room Sharing

———

I want to give a big thank you to everyone who works in hospitals.

I could never do what you do in the medical profession as I am terrified of all things medical. However, my aunt was a doctor, you see, and I witnessed some of the things she did, and well, I found it quite creepy, not to mention I don't know; I wouldn't say I like hospitals.

Probably because you know people are sick there, and people get operations and stuff I don't know. I find it all quite scary, and I mean.

I guess some people like, you know, fixing people and knowing what the inside of your body looks like, but that's just something that I don't enjoy like I like horror movies. I do not like ghoul-like things, and I don't enjoy watching people get their limbs cut off and stuff. So I, no, I don't. So yeah, hospitals make me think of that and cringe. So I find it quite scary probably; the terrifying place I can think of is a hospital.

Anyway, I didn't get a whole night's sleep, I'm not blaming my kid brother, she's a child after all, but you know he didn't sleep very well either, and I had a mega headache the whole next day, so yeah, my mind was not ready to tell some stories yesterday, but today, I am ready.

You see, when I was ten years old, I was in the hospital for a week. I won't go into the gory details about why I was there.

One night, my first night, I was settling down the late evening. I was fortunate enough to have a room to myself, although there was another bed opposite me, which was empty.

It must have been about 9 pm; the door opened, and a nurse brought in a male perhaps slightly older than me, maybe in his early teens. They settled him into his bed, and no one visited as it was very late after visiting hours.

When the nurse left, I waited a few minutes and said hello to him. But he sat there in the semi-darkness staring at the wall. As I had turned off my lamp, the only light in the room was from outside.

I then asked him if he was okay, and he replied, "I'm going to kill you tonight."

Well, I was terrified and stayed silent. I placed the blanket over my mouth and kept peeping out at him from over my blanket in the semi-lit room. The teenager didn't turn to look at me.

How was I going to sleep in that room? No way, I needed to do something fast. Then, after what must have been ten minutes, which seemed more like an hour to me, he repeated it!

No way, so I pressed my call button for assistance and kept my finger on it until a nurse came rushing into the room asking me if everything was alright.

I told her it was not "alright" and to get me out of there fast because this patient had threatened to kill me tonight! What the hell.

The nurse quickly shouted to another nurse for assistance. Finally, they got the teen out of my room and into another room. He was still sitting up in bed but now with his legs dangling off the side of the bed.

That night I could not sleep. I must have fallen off in the early hours of the morning.

Suddenly, I could feel my blanket tugged at. I felt as if someone was sitting on my bed. I felt a slight pressure on my legs. I woke up in a start. I must have been dreaming.

I telephoned for a nurse. It must have been about 5 am. When she entered the room, I told her what had happened earlier and asked the nurse - what if he came into my room later that night? I had asked the nurse this when she returned fifteen minutes after taking the teen away to another room earlier on.

The duty nurse then told me that the teen wouldn't be returning. He was blind, and he had no legs from the knee downwards.

Dementia Patients

———

We had a patient who told me that her deceased spouse was in the room with us to take her home.

I attempted to gently remind her that there was no one else in the room with us, but she insisted that her husband was there and that he'd want to take her home that evening after the kids left, whatever.

I dismissed it as senility nonsense and reasoned that if she's happy in this false notion, I'm so glad, but her kids and grandkids came to visit that day, and after they went, she peacefully passed away.

Even thinking about it gives me goosebumps to this day.

Ghost Stories

———

When I first started working at the hospital, the charge nurse on the oncology ward, with whom I became friends, told me some ghost stories. For example, he claimed that people started to report seeing a tiny child with bandages wrapped around his skull in the paediatric ward, and they would die a day or two later.

It sounded like a typical run-of-the-mill ghost story until I was working on the floor across the hospital one day. I had this patient whose condition was not improving, an older man with heart failure and arrhythmia at one point. So during the day, I go into this man's room, and he says to me, all of you need to do something about this little boy that keeps on coming in here.

Since I hadn't seen any kids running around, I asked him who he was talking about? He said the boy with all the bandages wrapped around his head!

My heart sunk to my stomach, and I looked around the run, somewhat excited but scared as well since I had never experienced anything like that.

I asked him if he had said anything to the little boy? And the older man said that he the little boy wears a cap and sticks his head out the wall, up there look. The older man then points and says that the cheeky boy then smiles at him and asks him if his pacemaker's working?

The older man again pointed to the upper back corner of the room near the ceiling.

I was so relieved there was no boy there and told the older man that I was sorry to say nothing was there. But, I can say one hundred per cent that I so freaked out!

The older man didn't see the boy again to my knowledge, but when I came back the following day, he had been transferred to the ICU overnight, and that is the only time in my life I have ever truly believed or come close to experiencing a ghost story.

About The Author

———

Granger T Barr lives in London with his wife and his dog. He has researched paranormal activities and real-life stories locally and around the world.

Thanks again for downloading your book. If you enjoyed reading this, please give us the thumbs-up.

Your feedback is important to us.

You may be interested in reading other books by Granger T Barr.

Other Books by This Author

––––––

Y*ou may be interested in other books within the Ghostly Encounters Series*:

True Ghost Stories and Hauntings: Real-Life Personal Short Ghost Stories In And Around Britain

13 short ghost stories

Real Ghost Stories and Hauntings: True-Life Short Ghost Stories (Ghostly Paranormal Encounters)

19 short ghost stories

True Ghost Stories & Hauntings Chilling Tales For Adults: Real Life Paranormal Ghostly Supernatural Encounters Collection From Around The World.

Don't miss out!

Visit the website below and you can sign up to receive emails whenever Granger T Barr publishes a new book. There's no charge and no obligation.

https://books2read.com/r/B-A-MMUL-EAGVB

Connecting independent readers to independent writers.

Also by Granger T Barr

Ghostly Encounters
True Ghost Stories and Hauntings
Real Ghost Stories and Hauntings
Ghost Stories Collection
True Ghost Stories And Hauntings: Chilling Tales For Adults:
Real Life Paranormal Ghostly Supernatural Encounters
Collection From Around The World
Real Ghosts, True-Life Stories, And Hauntings: Paranormal
Ghostly Supernatural Encounters
Haunted Hospitals: True Real Hospital Ghost Stories &
Hauntings 25 Unexplained Supernatural Mysteries Of The
Paranormal In Britain And America

CPSIA information can be obtained
at www.ICGtesting.com
Printed in the USA
LVHW111255180522
719112LV00010B/85

9 798201 835224